ALTITUDE ADJUSTMENT

Emily Eddins

© 2014 Emily Eddins
All Rights Reserved.

No part of this publication may be reproduced, stored in a retrieval system, or transmitted, in any form or by any means, electronic, mechanical, photocopying, recording, or otherwise, without the written permission of the author.

First published by Dog Ear Publishing
4010 W. 86th Street, Ste H
Indianapolis, IN 46268
www.dogearpublishing.net

ISBN: 978-1-4575-2755-5

This book is printed on acid-free paper.

Printed in the United States of America

For Lance

With Gratitude

Thank you to the following literary journals for allowing me to reprint my work. First, to the *Louisville Review* for allowing me to reprint my essay "News Junkie." Thank you also to *Forge* for allowing me to reprint my essay "Will It Work Out?" Thank you to *Toad Suck Review* for allowing me to reprint my essay "Gods and Whores."

Finally, I want to express my deep gratitude to all of my family and friends who have encouraged me along the way. I love you.

"If you want to tell people the truth, make them laugh, otherwise they'll kill you."

- Oscar Wilde

Disclaimer

The events in this book are mainly true. Some names have been changed to protect people who didn't know that one day I would be writing a book about them.

Contents

News Junkie 1

Will It Work Out? 11

Cabin Fever 27

It's Lonely at the Top 43

Gods and Whores 57

Are We Having Fun Yet? 69

Truckee Time 79

Moving On 89

News Junkie

Wolf Blitzer screams at me. His urgent voice wails like a siren through our sparsely furnished living room. Bored and on baby duty in our corporate apartment, I watch CNN around the clock. If I stare at the screen long enough, I see every news program at least three times. Test me: I can repeat each broadcast word for word and lip-synch to every reporter.

I dislike Wolf for a couple of reasons. The first is that there's just something weird about him. Don't you find it odd that he also actually resembles a wolf? Were his parents joking or just prescient when they named him? It's not his fault, but he gets on my nerves. We spend too much time together. He is on TV so often that he must actually live at CNN. I bet he sleeps in a Wolf-sized custom-made dog bed under the news desk. Since he doesn't have the kind of hair you have to brush (because it is wolf fur), he sleeps in his suit and pops straight up when his shift starts so he can immediately deliver all of the world's bad news (just like he did yesterday, and just like he will again tomorrow).

The second and the main reason that I dislike Wolf is that he reminds me too much of myself. He spends his whole day panicking about terrorists, anthrax, and snipers. Hmmm. Sounds familiar. As I lie wide-eyed, staring at the ceiling at three a.m., I imagine Wolf climbing into his little bed, closing his little wolf eyelids, and drifting off to sleep. I am jealous. I have not slept the night through since we moved to Washington, DC, a month earlier, on the one-year anniversary of 9/11. Unfortunately, not all of my insomnia can be blamed on my six-month-old son waking up at two a.m. to scream at me, Wolf Blitzer-style. (Is it because he hears Wolf all day long that he has adopted an almost identical, piercing timbre?) No, it has more to do with the fact that Washington, DC, is a war zone. Outside of my bedroom window, missile launchers wait expectantly on the sidewalk. Soldiers patrol the streets with big, scary guns. And as if that weren't enough to rattle me, Wolf reports that someone is driving around the city in a white box truck, shooting people at random.

"A sniper," he bellows, "targeting innocent people!"

I live right in the middle of a giant bull's-eye, a feeling I can't seem to shake even when I am safely locked in my apartment (which is most of the time). My baby, Wilson, sleeps all day long, and I do not know enough about being a mother yet to realize that I can actually wake him up and take him out, so Wolf and I sit around and feed off of each other. He needs an audience, and I need noise. Even if nothing is happening in my apartment, somewhere in the world, life is interesting, and scary. I can't change the channel, because I need the adrenaline rush that twenty-four-hour news provides.

On bad days, I am trapped in the apartment with CNN until around four p.m. because I haven't gotten my act together quickly enough to get Wilson out of the apartment before he needs another nap. If he sleeps too long, I pace the apartment in loops, willing him to rouse himself. We don't have much furniture, so I walk in a big circle, cruising from room to room. I stop to check my e-mail account. Sadly, I actually have time to read the long chains of joke e-mails that my (also bored) mother sends me. I crack open a can of soda. I gaze out the large, industrial windows, into the grey October skyline. It is not even winter yet, but outside, it is as dreary as a corpse. We will be in this city, in this antiseptic apartment, until March—a sentence that feels too long to bear.

On good days, I get out before ten in the morning and Wilson and I walk around town for a little while before I have to bring him back up to our seventh-floor apartment for his nap. My morning mission is to try to find an adult to talk to: someone, anyone. It could be a dry cleaner or the clerk at the drugstore; I don't mind. I don't have any real friends in DC because we are only here for a few months. It seems like a waste of time to put effort into finding people I actually relate to, only to leave them, so I rely on the kindness of strangers to get me by. The employees at Safeway are paid to be friendly, so sometimes I go grocery shopping for friends, lingering to chat with the produce stocker or the cashier.

"How you doing today, Emily?" the doorman asks as Wilson and I leave the apartment building on one of our little jaunts.

"Just fine, thank you!" He cheers me up because he is one of the few people in DC who knows my name. "How are you, Mega?" I cheer him up because I know his name, too. "What's up with all the policemen parked outside?" I ask.

"We are now at Code Orange," he cautions.

"Oh! Is that because of the sniper, the impending dirty bomb, or the anthrax alert?" I laugh nervously. Wilson looks up at me and smiles innocently. If he understood what we were talking about, he would be crying his head off. I consider going back upstairs for a second but decide to take my chances against the sniper. After all, he could aim and miss, but if I don't get out of the building, cabin fever will definitely kill me.

I head for the drugstore. Maybe Rita the cashier will be there today. She's always up for a conversation. I am on a mission to buy duct tape because the Department of Homeland Security has warned me I will need to tape up our apartment windows in the event of a dirty-bomb explosion. I envision my darling baby son gagging on nuclear fallout and decide to take his advice.

"Hi there," Rita exclaims as I walk into the drugstore.

"How *are* you, Rita?" I ask with a little too much enthusiasm. She's practically my best friend. She's looking frail and seems a little smaller than usual. Perhaps the weight of my social desperation is crushing her.

"I've got the gout!" she confides.

"Oh, I'm sorry," I console. I am not exactly sure what the gout is, but it sounds medieval and like it may involve pus, so I don't question her further. "I'm here for some duct tape," I say to change the subject.

"Oh God! That Tom Ridge," she complains. "We're completely sold out."

"Sold out!" My heart hammers in my chest. I have left it too late, and now Wilson will die a horrific and painful death, developing radioactive thyroid tumors and slowly wasting away in my arms.

"How about packing tape?" I ask Rita, praying she'll say that it will definitely prevent radioactive particles from seeping into our apartment.

"Well, I guess that might work," she says. "It's thick!"

I clear the shelf, buying ten rolls and leaving none for my negligent but mentally stable neighbors who are clearly not worried about death by fallout.

"The others will have to use Scotch tape!" I announce recklessly, only half joking.

"People sure are crazy!" Rita proclaims.

I am not sure if that remark is pointed at me, at the terrorists, or at Tom Ridge. Are we all becoming equally crazy? I take my tape up to the counter, stick my tail between my legs, and race Wilson home.

Scanning the street for white box trucks, I breathe a sigh of relief as I enter my building. We will live to see another day.

"I can't wait to get the hell out of here!" I announce to Mega on the way inside.

"Yes, ma'am," he answers. They have trained the doormen to be agreeable, and this is his standard response to everything.

If I said, "I hope you kissed your wife this morning, because this building could be blown up today," he would reply, "Yes, ma'am."

When my husband, Lance, walks in the door that night, I am ecstatic that the sniper did not kill him on the way home.

"You're alive!" I scream, pouncing on him.

"Well, you are easy to please!" he chuckles.

He does not seem to realize that he has cheated death, for now. But if the sniper doesn't slay him, the corporate world eventually might. He looks so tired—the long commutes, the business travel, and the interminable evenings at the office are wearing him down.

"I can't wait to get out of here," he says quietly. "Everything will be better in California."

In a few months, we are moving to a little ski town called Truckee in the mountains of Northern California.

I know that life will be safer and simpler there for us and, most importantly, for Wilson. I want him to grow up knowing his neighbors, not fearing that someone is going to shoot him while he is walking to school or going to bomb his home one random afternoon.

I can't wait to live in a small town that Osama bin Laden has never heard of. Who would set off a dirty bomb in a town with a population of 14,000? In Truckee, there are no high-rises for planes to crash into, and the only public transportation to target is a little van that shuttles residents to the ski slopes. We will be safe there. I just know it.

I put the TV on mute. Wolf Blitzer mouths something and looks invigorated. It's as if the constant stream of adrenaline the terrorist threats supply makes him a little high, and he likes it. I suspect that I too am addicted to the drama of it all: the buzz of fear I feel when I see a new video released by Al Qaeda. The bearded men in their turbans talking about how happy they will be when they kill us all, about how we should watch our backs because they are planning something even bigger and more horrible than 9/11. They want to scare me. And it works.

To the terrorists, I am a target. To CNN, I am a target of a different sort: a viewer. The anchors and the terrorists have a symbiotic relationship. If the terrorists did not have a twenty-four-hour simulcast megaphone, their ability to frighten would be drastically reduced. If the anchors didn't have frightening news to report, their audience would be greatly reduced.

    I vow to keep the TV turned off tomorrow. I am going to tune out the noise: the anchor chatter, the terrorist chatter, all of it. No matter how bored, how desperate I become, I am going to quit CNN and fear, cold turkey. Maybe I will run over to Rite-Aid and check on Rita's gout. Now that's scary.

Will It Work Out?

As young urbanites living in Washington, DC, my husband, Lance, and I often mused about what it would be like to live in one of our favorite vacation spots in California. Idling behind other drivers on our painful commute to towering office buildings, we dreamed of ditching this way of life and moving to Truckee, a ski town surrounded by snow-capped mountains and blue alpine lakes. While living on the East Coast, I met a lot of people who dreamed of one day moving to California, but now that I live in California, I have never met a single person who dreams of one day moving to the East Coast. Californians are smugly confident that they live in the most beautiful state in the nation. This certainty creeps east and infects people living elsewhere with the nagging idea that until they move west, they might just be missing out on something.

The western dream nagged at us (or perhaps I just nagged at Lance), so much that we eventually did pack up our family and head west on a quest for the good life. We trusted that Truckee would be the balm to soothe our harried urban souls. After all, we had vacationed there for years, visiting my sister, Sarah, and her family, who lived in the neighborhood where we had just bought a house.

Within a week of living in our new environment, I realized that being a permanent resident of this vacation spot felt entirely different than being a visitor. I was out of place: an uptight, marginally athletic urbanite inhabiting a sleepy town populated mainly by former Olympians. My daily life became a sociological experiment. Would I be able to adapt to this chronically relaxed way of life? Would my family not only survive but thrive in this cold and alien world? Would our cross-country, modern-day pioneer migration actually work out? I felt like a lab rat in a snowy psych lab.

I was surprised that Lance and I abandoned our city ways as easily as if we were stepping out of business suits and into exercise clothes. For example, in Truckee, I suddenly felt absolutely no pressure to bathe. When we lived in the city, I got up, washed my hair, put on makeup, and got dressed. I had to be presentable because everyone else was. In Truckee, it isn't apparent that anyone bathes too much. And nobody ever wears nice clothes—even to weddings. People pretty much wear the same thing: shorts, a T-shirt, and sandals in the summer. In the winter, jeans and a fleece.

I can get away with not bathing, at least for a little while. My husband cannot but thinks he can. In all the years we lived in the city, his hygiene was never an issue. He got up, took a shower, put on clean underwear, got dressed, and went to work. When we moved to Truckee, he gave all this up.

"Honey," I said, "aren't you going to take a shower?"

"Why?" he replied. "I'm not going to see anyone today."

"You're seeing me right now," I said.

"That doesn't count."

"It never occurred to me that the only reason you showered was because you had to go to work."

"Me neither," he said. "But I guess that was it."

After engaging in hard-core physical activity, however, he would usually bathe. Thus, I often encouraged him to work out, hoping it would result in a shower and a couple of blissful days of his smelling fresh.

"Working out" is the main activity of everyone we know in Truckee. In the city, "working out" means going to the gym. In Truckee, "working out" generally means, but is not limited to, running straight up the side of a mountain for at least two hours with no breaks, cross-country skiing straight up the side of a mountain for at least two hours with no breaks, or mountain biking straight down the side of a mountain for at least two hours with no brakes. In Truckee, working out is not just something people do for fun; it is the central organizing principle of life.

"When are you going to the grocery store?" one might ask a spouse.

"After my workout," any spouse would respond.

"When are you going to make funeral arrangements for your mother?" a friend might ask someone who has just lost a parent.

"After my workout," the bereaved would respond.

In the city, when you meet someone at a party and begin to chat, the conversation usually moves toward finding out what the other person does for a living. It is the essential thing you need to know because it defines the other human being. While just as shallow, random and frustrating as the Truckee athletic worthiness criteria, learning what someone does for a living is similar in that it is what people use to get to the heart of the matter. By this, I mean they use it to determine whether that person has an interesting job and is therefore an interesting person, whether that person has a lucrative job and is therefore wealthy, or whether that person may be a potential friend or may be valuable to you as a business contact and thus worthy of further conversation.

In Truckee, what one does for a living is secondary. In fact, it is not apparent what most people do for a living, even after you have known them for an extended time. Because people live to "work out" rather than live to work, what is apparent in Truckee is whether you are an athlete. In Truckee, if you do not work out, you do not exist; at parties, people see past you. Nobody knows your name.

It did not dawn on me until I lived here that athletic inadequacy would make me a social pariah, an anthropological curiosity. Attend any social event in Truckee, and you will quickly learn that working out is primary. Begin a conversation with a stranger, and before long, the person you are talking to will literally get to the heart of the matter. By this, I mean they will determine what your resting heart rate is; whether your resting heart rate is higher or lower than theirs;

whether you might be competition for them in a ski race, bike race, or the human race.

Once, I went to get a haircut from a woman named Shay in downtown Truckee. An acquaintance suggested I call her, and against my better judgment, I made an appointment. Shay's salon was right next to the local grocery store, where I shopped at least three times a week. Every time I entered the grocery store with my shopping cart, I looked through her large plate-glass window and saw her inside. The reason I did not want to call her is that I inevitably have to fire my hairdressers, and I thought it might be awkward if we bumped into each other every time I went to the store for a gallon of milk. I have short hair, and if I run into a hairdresser I have stopped seeing after say, three months, it is obvious that my hair is still short and that I have covertly begun to see someone else. If this sounds a little like dating, well, it is. There is no polite way to break up with a hairdresser, so I take the direct approach and simply stop calling. Sooner or later, the hairdresser figures out I'm just not that into them.

I had never met Shay before I ventured into her salon. She came to the door beaming, still wearing her black Lycra tights and orange ski shirt from her morning workout. "Come in!" she squealed, her blue eyes watering. Upon meeting her, I immediately became suspicious. Why was she so happy to see me? Was I the first client she had seen in a while? I grew increasingly concerned when I saw the miniature fire truck installed in front of the large mirror where she worked.

"Am I supposed to sit on that?" I asked.

"Oh, I have a chair in the closet," she said, rushing over to get it.

Quickly, I surmised that I was probably the only adult customer in a long time and that I would likely leave her salon with a haircut similar to a four-year-old boy's. I did not feel any better when I studied the condition of Shay's very maroon, almost purple, hair and determined she was probably cutting it herself and using a hairstyle catalogue from 1985 as a guide.

We commenced with the horribly painful get-to-know-you chitchat one must endure while getting one's hair cut for the first time. I wish there were a little badge you could wear that said, "I don't mean to be rude. I just want to sit here in silence while you cut my hair." I wish this badge were socially acceptable and readily available for purchase at any convenience store in America. But it is not, so I chatted.

"So, how many kids do you have?" she asked.

"One boy who is one year old," I responded. "That makes coming to get my haircut a real luxury! Please excuse me if I fall asleep in your chair." (Hint! Hint! Don't make me talk! I just want to stare blankly into space!) She did not catch on, and kept talking. Just two questions into the conversation, she got to the heart of the matter.

"So," she said expectantly, "do you ski?"

"Sure," I replied, like a typical novice flatlander.

"So do you do any of the races around here? The Gold Rush? The Skogsloppet? What's your best time?"

"Oh … you mean cross-country ski," I replied.

"Duh!" She laughed, as if there were any other kind of skiing.

At the time, I did not realize but have since come to learn that downhill skiing is not viewed as a workout by the locals. It is considered a form of amusement but does not result in a sufficient enough increase in heart rate to be considered exercise.

"Oh a little, not really," I muttered, diminished. "I like to downhill."

"Slalom? Moguls?" she replied indifferently. Clearly, I would not be racing in her division and thus did not merit further conversation.

"No, easy stuff. Mostly groomed greens and gentle blues," I responded, as though in a foreign language. I could see Shay's reflection in the mirror suppressing a smile. Silence ensued, except for the water dripping in her kid-sized sink.

A few weeks later, my sister took me out to the cross-country center for one of her "lessons." She was my only friend in Truckee, and I realized that if I wanted to spend time with her, I would have to learn how to cross-country ski. Since childhood, I have been her project. She is convinced that if she leaves me stranded in enough athletically compromising situations, eventually, I will discover my hidden inner Olympian. After more than thirty years, this has not yet happened, but she remains undeterred. My four-year-old niece, Alice, was tagging along. Apparently, the runs I would be skiing were a little easy for her, but she was feeling charitable. When I suggested we all go to the neighborhood downhill center instead, my sister looked at me with horror. "We don't want Alice to downhill until she's a teenager," she replied. "We are afraid it will make her lazy."

Even though Sarah always encourages me to go to the cross-country center, I can tell the whole idea of having me on her turf makes her slightly nervous. We are the exact same height and weight, and we both have short blonde hair. We look so similar (when we are not skiing) that people often mistake us for one another. When I am on skis, flailing all over the meadow, wiping out and otherwise embarrassing myself, I think she is worried sick that someone will confuse me for her. In her dreams at night, she must imagine gossip ripping through the ski shop like wildfire. "Did you see Sarah out there? She must be really out of shape!" (In Truckee, calling someone out of shape is about the worst insult you could deliver.)

My sister has skied every day of every ski season since 1989. I will never and could never look as good as she does on skis. For her, it is effortless. If my Olympian is hiding somewhere inside me, hers is on display for everyone to see; therefore, I feel a lot of pressure to look like I know what I am doing so I won't embarrass her. I literally exhaust myself trying to be something I am not. It's possible I was Chinese in another life, I try so hard to avoid bringing shame on her. But I am simply not a skier, try as I may, so it's inevitable that I will embarrass her as well as myself. It's already happened once, and almost twice.

The first time it happened the day started out well. I had skied my personal best, somehow managing to finish the route my sister had laid out for me, without injury and with only minor curse words muttered quietly under my breath. Smiling, I felt myself skiing in slow motion to the mental tune of "We Are the Champions" as I glided up to the lodge and snapped out of my bindings.

"I am looking good!" I told myself as I walked into the restaurant to reward myself with a snack. My crumpled dollar bill was placed triumphantly in the hand of the Argentinean teenager who had traveled to Truckee to work at the lodge expressly for the purpose of helping me enjoy this special cup of hot cocoa on this particular golden day. I held the steaming cup to my lips, swallowed and crack! My front tooth exploded! Apparently, I had been smiling a little too much and my high-deductible, out of network, porcelain crown had frozen in my mouth. It shattered the second it was hit by a wave of hot chocolate. I rushed to the mirror over the condiment bar and nervously opened my mouth. It was as I had feared. A jack-o-lantern in a ski hat stared back at me. I spent the rest of my vacation racing back and forth to the dentist, avoiding hot drinks, and pretending I was not the toothless lady who had cried all the way from the lodge, to the parking shuttle bus, to her car. For the rest of the season, people came up to my sister asking if she had recovered from her dental explosion.

The second time I almost brought shame on my sister occurred the winter before we moved to Truckee. Lance and I were out cross-country skiing. He was far in front of me, and I was trying to catch up. We were on a flat, supposedly easy trail. I hit a patch of ice, and the next thing I knew, my right leg rotated 180 degrees until the back of my knee was where my kneecap should have been. My physical agony was outweighed only by my embarrassment. Though I was hurt, all I could think was that I had to avoid being seen. I tried to drag myself off the trail and into the woods. I now understand why dogs leave their backyards and wander off to die.

Not a minute elapsed before an impossibly tall man dressed in black from head to toe and wearing reflective glasses skied up and offered to help. Maybe he seemed impossibly tall because I was lying prostrate on the ground with a noodle for a leg.

"I'll go back to the lodge and get ski patrol to bring a snowmobile to rescue you," he said with a deep voice that sounded like Superman's. He was dying to play superhero and was already halfway to the lodge before I had a chance to protest.

I have to act fast! I thought. *If I ride back to the lodge in one of those stretchers, I'll never live it down.* And then the realization hit me harder than the impact of my fall: *Sarah will never live it down! Everyone will think* she *injured herself and had to be rescued.* My heart raced as I tried to figure a way out of my predicament. I struggled like an animal in a trap to make my injured leg move. Realizing I would never get far on my own, I was relieved to turn around and see Lance heading for me. As he approached, he saw that the slumped form on the edge of the trail was his wife.

"I thought you were a tree stump!" he exclaimed.

Tears rolled down my cheeks.

"Oh my God!" he said. "Are you hurt?"

"Don't worry about that!" I wailed, panicked. "You've got to drag me off this trail! A man has gone to get ski patrol, and they are going to haul me back to the lodge in one of those orange sleds!"

"Oh no!" he said, trying not to laugh. He dragged me into a grove of trees, where we hid while the snowmobile droned back and forth, searching for wounded prey like a buzzard.

"Please don't let them find me," I whispered under my breath. By the grace of God, they did not, and Lance helped me limp back to the car. Physically but not socially injured, I had escaped family shame—barely.

So this ski season, I had settled upon a new strategy. Instead of trying to improve my skiing, my main goal was to avoid embarrassing myself, and, more importantly, my sister, by sticking to the easy trails and spending as much time as possible taking breaks and sipping out of my water bottle. A few minutes after Alice and my sister had given up on me, I saw Shay skiing toward me in her trademark orange shirt. I thought perhaps we would pretend we didn't recognize each other because we were both hidden in ski hats, Lycra tights, and glasses. I was still bitter about the preschool haircut she had given me and was considering wearing my ski hat (even when I was not skiing) for the next couple of months. The breakup was coming sooner than I'd expected, and here was the awkward moment that I had prophesied. I stopped to drink some water so she would not see what a bad skier I was.

"Oh, hi, Emily. I didn't realize you worked out!" Shay trilled as she zoomed past. From her actions, I could tell that she did not deem me to be a "stopping friend." In Truckee, a stopping friend is someone whom you actually like enough to stop your workout to speak to.

"Call me when you need a trim!" she yelled.

"I don't think so," I muttered to her trailing figure, now in the distance. "It's just not working out."

Cabin Fever

By abandoning our city lives in Washington, DC, and moving to the ski town of Truckee, Lance and I were part of a small but growing trend of yuppies intent on ruralization—escaping urban environments to chase a bucolic dream. We felt confident we would love living year-round in such a beautiful mountain town, and I was especially excited about living closer to my sister, Sarah.

Though Sarah and I were both born and raised in Alabama, she got the hell out as soon as she was eighteen. She headed west by herself, in my father's old lime-green Mercury. She came back to Alabama to visit a few times while I was growing up, and each time, she seemed weirder than the last. When she was a teenager in Alabama, she was the star of the high school tennis team, wore lots of makeup, and modeled for a local department store. After she moved to California, she stopped shaving her legs, quit wearing makeup, and refused to eat meat. Her transformation was my first impression of California. Judging by how alien my sister became to me, I thought the Golden State was practically a foreign country.

The first time I visited her in Northern California, I was seventeen. I saw that there were more women who didn't shave their legs, wear makeup, or eat meat, thus confirming my earlier suspicion that my sister was not the only one behaving this way. On my first visit, I tried sushi for the first time, drank espresso for the first time, and used a fake ID for the first time. I realized that everything that was cool in America happened in California first and then spread east, reaching the South about fifteen years later.

I did not want to wait that long for more sushi and lattes, so I decided I needed to live in California. In the end, it took me a while to get there—exactly fifteen years. Apparently, everything that is uncool in the South takes fifteen years to reach California.

So I found myself at the age of thirty-two, with my husband and son, living in our new home perched on the edge of a cliff at an altitude of about 7,000 feet in Truckee. We had bought our dream house (in the back corner of a 1970's era subdivision — but we thought it was cool)! On sunny days, a panoramic view of the Sierra Nevada mountain range stretched in every direction, but shortly after we moved in, we experienced our first real blizzard. We could barely see a foot in front of us. It was snowing so hard, it was difficult to see where the road ended and our yard began. Pregnant with our second son and carrying our one-year-old little boy on my hip, I ventured outside and felt like a pioneer woman trudging through two feet of fresh snow on the driveway. The neighborhood snowplow had visited earlier in the day, but its nozzle had piled snow at least eight feet high on either side of the driveway. Pelting down in hard sheets like heavy rain, the snow was still falling and wouldn't let up any time soon. The sky was dark with heavy clouds.

I ran back inside when I heard the phone ringing. It was my sister. "Have you seen the blob?" she asked.

"The what?" I asked. This was the first of many weather-related colloquialisms in Truckee that I would come to learn.

"The blob!" she shrieked. "On the Weather Channel—the huge, green satellite image of precipitation covering the entire state of California. It is by far the biggest blob I have seen since at least the winter of 1997, and that turned out to be the most powdery, gigantic dump of all time."

If someone in the city had waxed so enthusiastic about an impending dump, I would have been disgusted by her vulgarity, but in Truckee, hearing that a dump is on the horizon is the best news anyone could hope to receive. It means a giant snowstorm is imminent.

"Whoa!" I said, trying to get excited, too. "How long is it supposed to last?"

"At least two more days, hopefully four," she said. "Oops—I have to run now. It's Local on the 8's. I'll call you back."

Every eight minutes on the Weather Channel, you hear your latest local weather update. In Truckee, if you call someone at 8:58 or 9:08 or any eight, they will not answer the phone. They are watching Local on the 8's. Truckeeites monitor every drop in barometric pressure, every storm front building off of Asia, with intense anticipation. Go to any coffee shop, any bar, or, well—any place at all—and a twenty-four-hour weather station blasts its prediction across a crowd of hopeful skiers. Scan any local paper, and the headlines read either "No snow in forecast" or "Giant storm headed our way from Japan."

That evening, because we were officially residents of Truckee, Lance and I watched the Weather Channel.

The blob was giant and green and pretty much stalling out right on top of our house. Unlike my sister, I couldn't watch a stagnant green blob for hours on end. I needed more variety! Watching the Weather Channel was a slippery slope for me. It was only two channels over from CNN. With a mere flick of the "up" button on our remote control, I would be hooked again. I had been on the wagon for only about a week, but the lure of twenty-four-hour news coverage was proving too irresistible to escape. I could no more give up CNN than I could other vices like chocolate or soda. It was the perfect mind-numbing opiate. I fell back into my old routine instantly.

"Hi, Wolf!" I said to the TV. "Did you miss me?"

My anchor friends seemed even more interesting than before I had given them up. What's more, now I had a real friend to share them with! I had brought Lance over to the dark side, and the two of us watched cable news until we passed out in front of the TV. I had always heard that shared interests make a marriage work, and though I wasn't sure that a marriage therapist would qualify cable news addiction as something that would necessarily strengthen our relationship, it was fun to have someone to snuggle with while Wolf yelled at me.

I woke up in the middle of the night on the sofa to the sound of the wind howling. The plate glass in our living room windows sucked in and then breathed out, as if it were alive. The roof shuddered, the walls creaked, and each new gust increasingly convinced me that the storm would chew up our house and spit it right down the side of the mountain.

"Honey! Get up. The house is going to explode!" I tugged at Lance's arm to wake him.

"Man, it's really getting nasty out there," he observed. "But don't worry. The house is engineered to handle this kind of storm." He put his head back on the sofa cushion and promptly resumed snoring.

I ran into the bedroom and climbed into bed. The bedroom windows heaved louder than the windows had in the living room. The room was cold and so dark that I couldn't make out any of the furniture. Even though I was tucked into bed, I felt far too close to the elements for my own comfort. My mind raced as fast as the wind. What in the hell were we doing living on the edge of a mountain, anyway? Perhaps our house was no longer secured to the cliff at all. Perhaps the super-engineered pilings had blown loose and our first storm here would be the last we'd ever see. I shut my eyes and imagined my dream home falling end over end off the side of the mountain, my precious baby, my sleeping husband, and I spinning like clothes in a dryer amongst the granite countertops, stainless appliances, and log accents.

The house shook and rumbled as gusts pounded against it like battering rams. "It's engineered for this! It's engineered for this!" I repeated over and over, as if counting sheep, until I fell asleep.

The next morning, I woke up at 5:57 and ran to the TV so I could catch Local on the 8's. The forecast: snow—lots of it. The weatherman was predicting up to four more feet that day. Local on the 8's ended. The phone rang. It was Sarah.

"Woo-hoo!" she yelled, elated. "Did you *see* that *freaking* blob?"

"Did I ever," I responded, trying to conceal my worry. "Woo-hoo!"

"I totally wanna come see you, but it's snowing too hard," she said. "Gotta go—it's almost 6:08."

It snowed nonstop the rest of that day, and the day after that. On the fourth day of the storm, I woke to find the snow piled up higher than our front door. We were certifiably trapped, and I felt certifiably crazy. Unease accumulated inside me with each flake. My sanity dangled off the edge of our panoramic view deck, but I couldn't leave the house to retrieve it. Every word my husband said, every sound my baby made grated on me. For the first time, I understood the phrase "crawling out of your skin." I wanted to run away and do something luxurious like drive to the grocery store or hang out at the gym. I just needed to go somewhere and be alone, but there was nowhere to *be* alone. A scream was building inside me, and I could do nothing to stifle it.

It was no coincidence that during the blizzard, Lance (who is normally my favorite person) seemed to be demonstrating irritating behaviors more frequently than usual. One of the nasty habits he had acquired in the past three days was playing Eric Clapton tunes on Wilson's toy guitar. Hearing "Layla" played 4,000 times in a row on an out-of-tune children's ukulele would put anyone in an insane asylum.

I saw him pick up the guitar and gave him a poisonous look. He quietly put it down. I wandered into a room and forgot why I was there. I looked in the mirror at myself and inspected the dried baby food on the lapel of my flannel pajamas. I had been wearing them for at least two days, maybe more. I couldn't remember. What day was it, anyway? I squinted hard, trying to remember, but couldn't. We had lapsed into wearing our pajamas all day long because there was really no point in getting dressed. We napped all day long because there was nothing else to do. We suffered from too much sleep and too little hygiene. The only remarkable thing that had happened for two straight days was that Wilson had uttered his first word, but my joy had quickly turned to guilt when I'd understood the word he was actually trying to say.

"Baghdad!" He looked up at me and gurgled with an innocent expression.

Now I know how a meth addict feels when she wakes up from her binge to realize her child has been left to wallow in a dirty diaper in his crib all day. My son's first word was one he had picked up from the secondhand smoke of my CNN addiction! Baghdad! Oh, no one will ever know the depths of my shame. Wilson was hooked, too! The overwhelming guilt forced me to finally turn off the TV. Afterward, Wilson cried edgily, as if going through withdrawal.

The days flowed like one big, long run-on sentence with no end and no beginning. I needed punctuation. I needed to get dressed. Go out. Do something. Come home. Eat dinner. Go to bed. On the fourth day, I got up, took a shower, and got dressed. I ate breakfast, bathed my son, and dressed him. I pretended that our house was not turning into a giant igloo. I told myself I was staying home because I had important work to do. Lance watched the baby while I searched for a purpose. I cleaned the crumbs out of the utensil drawer. I shoveled ash from the fireplace. I vacuumed under the rugs and searched for loose change between sofa cushions. I could not control my external environment, so I desperately organized our internal one.

After watching all my activity, Lance asked me to hold the baby so he could take a shower. Apparently, he had been vicariously breaking a sweat with me all morning. I halted my important work and fed Wilson lunch. I put him in his crib for a nap and resisted lying down on the carpet next to him. There would be no more carpet prints on my face! I was turning over a new leaf.

I picked up a book by David Lavender called *Snowbound, The Tragic Story of the Donner Party*, about a group of emigrants who got stuck in what is now Truckee during the winter of 1846. This book was probably not the most calming choice of reading material during a blizzard, but I had already read everything else in the house, including all of the old newspapers we had originally saved for starting fires.

I was desperate for entertainment, but I was not as desperate as the Donners. If you ever want to make yourself feel better, remind yourself that there were once people so hungry and cold that they ate leather and lived in underground snow caves for months on end. The winter the Donners were trapped was supposedly the snowiest winter in California history, though I was seriously wondering if this winter was going to top it.

By this point, the sliding glass door on our deck was completely encased in a giant drift. I couldn't see outside. I read on.

> *Realizing that they were stranded by snowdrifts over twenty feet high, the Donner Party erected cabins along Truckee Lake at the end of October. The cattle had all been killed and eaten by mid-December; one man had died of malnutrition. The people began to eat bark, twigs, and boiled hides.*

Panic rose inside me as I pictured our house under a twenty-foot drift. Surely we were already halfway there. "Oh my God!" I screamed at Lance, asleep in the chair on the other side of the room. Much to my irritation, he seemed to be almost enjoying the blizzard, using it to catch up on the sleep he had missed by working late for the past seven years.

"What?" he said dreamily, completely out of it.

"We are going to die!" I cried. "Do you hear me? *Die*—trapped here in our house like the Donners."

I ran to the pantry to see how much food we had left. A quick inventory revealed a box of Special K, some baby food, and two cans of beans. We would not have to resort to bark and twigs just yet.

"Don't worry," said Lance. "Worst-case scenario, you can ski down to Safeway tomorrow and pick up some food."

"Yeah right," I said. If our dinner was dependent on my skiing ability, then starvation was a definite possibility! I continued to read.

> *Some of the survivors left in the camps had begun to eat the dead. It is believed that about half of the survivors of the Donner party resorted to cannibalism, having held off for as long as they could after their food was gone.*

I looked over at Lance. He was tall and muscular, without much fat on his body. I wasn't sure what he would taste like, but I would definitely have a hard time fitting him in the oven. Besides, I didn't think I could eat my husband even if I were starving to death. I knew him too well. It would be like eating your pet dog.

I looked outside. The snow swirled in mini tornadoes, hitting our kitchen window with a constant pinging sound that made it feel like we lived in a popcorn popper. After four days of snow assault, I was pretty sure Mother Nature hated my guts and derived sadistic pleasure from the constant stream of miniature snowballs she hurled at my face as I stared through the window. I had a new sympathy for fish in aquariums, tapping against the glass at the world outside. The snow painted the wooden siding on our house in a sticky powdery coating. I was like a little gingerbread woman glued in her sugar-coated cottage. Three-foot-long icicles hung down from the eaves of our porch like giant fangs waiting to puncture me.

The ringing phone interrupted my macabre thoughts. It was Sarah. She sounded depressed.

"What's wrong?" I asked.

"The storm is winding down," she said.

"How do you know?" I asked, relief washing over me like the rays of a tropical sun.

"I've cross-referenced the Local on the 8's forecast with the barometric pressure reading on the personal weather system on our deck, and double-checked it against the NOAA website. It's conclusive. The blob is dissipating."

At first, I thought I heard it. And then I was increasingly sure I heard it—the unmistakably lovely whine of a snowplow somewhere in the distance. It sounded almost like the roar of a distant airplane, and for a second, I was afraid it might be one, until I heard the "Beep! Beep! Beep!" of its reverse signal as it backed out of a driveway down the road. Through the swirling snow, I saw a faint red light flashing and making its way toward our house. The drone came closer until I saw the plow's giant nozzle spewing snow like a friendly dragon breathing thick steam.

"Here comes the plow!" I screamed. "We're saved! We're saved!"

"Oh well," Sarah said, consoling herself. "There's a tropical depression building off the coast of Malaysia."

I threw on my coat and a hat and ran outside for the first time in almost five days. Sarah was right. The blob was dissipating. The snow seemed lighter. I held my hand in front of my face to test my theory. I could see my fingers clearly. They were pink and wet. I looked down the street. Someone was shoveling snow off his porch, and smoke curled out of another house's chimney. There were other survivors! The one-story homes were completely buried, and two-story houses had snowdrifts up to the second-floor windows.

Breathing in my freedom, I realized I would not end up like the Donners. "Fire up those cans of beans!" I screamed to Lance. There would be no bark or twigs for dinner tonight, and I would not have to eat my neighbors. This pioneer had survived not only the storm but also torture by ukelele. My cabin fever had finally broken! Now it was time to dig out.

It's Lonely at the Top

I am sitting in Starbucks, trying to figure out exactly when I stopped being popular. It happened quietly and without fanfare. I'm not trying to brag, but being unpopular is a recent phenomenon for me. As I nurse my latte, my mind scrolls back to the beginning of my social life. Northington Elementary: I had two best friends, and a boyfriend from first to fifth grade. We were "going together" by virtue of several notes he had passed me stating (not asking!) as much, and my association with him automatically made me popular. We were, it's safe to say, an elementary school power couple. He was captain of the safety patrol, and I was a library assistant. He smelled of sweat and peanut butter. Every time I glanced at him across our crowded classroom, I caught him staring at me. His attention made me nervous, and it made me want to be near him. Our first kiss was on the playground in front of throngs of applauding admirers.

In middle school, I was actually voted "Most Popular," an honor made less illustrious by the fact that I campaigned heavily for it, making posters, buttons, and copious other election paraphernalia. This is the kind of "election" that no school in my new, progressive home state of California would ever sanction, but growing up in Alabama in the '70's, the campaign for "Most Popular" was as accepted as beauty pageants, baseball, and apple pie. As it turned out, my public push to be loved was time well spent, because my title carried me through to high school, where I found myself in the crowd I knew was considered cool. Now, let me clarify by saying I was never cool in a cheerleader or homecoming queen kind of way. Rather, I was in the group that considered themselves too cool to be cheerleaders or homecoming queens. We drank warm beer that we stole from our parents and stayed out all night partying. I assumed my star would continue to rise.

As I take the last swig of my coffee, I have a eureka moment: I was popular until I got married. Up until then, I shared houses and apartments with all my friends from college as we drank our way through our twenties in Washington, DC. Because it was easier to hang out with each other than to go out and make new friends, we successfully extended the shelf life of one another's popularity until we were thirty years old. There were so many of us who had gone to college together that we felt absolutely no need to meet new people and, in so doing, determine whether our popularity could survive in the real world. We simply prolonged our collegiate experience for a good six to eight years after graduation. Throwing parties, going out and staying up all night, we bonded over hangovers at breakfast and laughed about bad hookups just as we had when we were younger.

I can't blame my darling husband for the fact that my popularity took a nosedive after marriage, but I can pin its demise to the fact that shortly after we were married, we moved to London. And shortly after that, we moved back to our former stomping grounds in Washington, only to find that my friends from my post-college days had since dispersed and moved elsewhere to begin their adult lives. And shortly after that unsuccessful stint, we moved to Truckee. After the third move, I had successfully left behind every friend I'd ever known, and for the first time in my entire life, I felt certifiably lonely.

When you move to a place where nobody knows anything about you, you learn how hard it is to make friends, and how long it takes to make a really good one. Part of the problem is that you have to actually be a nicer, more sanitized version of yourself when meeting someone for the first time.

"Just be yourself!" you tell yourself. But then you hear the fine print being read in your head in that fast voice that states the disclaimer at the end of drug commercials: *When being yourself, do not be the real yourself, which includes foul-mouthed language, fits of melancholy, occasional neediness, radical left-wing politics, and a failure to accept different points of view. Only be yourself if you are sure the person you are talking to can handle the real yourself. Otherwise, be the vanilla version of yourself, which is more boring than the real yourself, yet more socially palatable.*

Perhaps the fact that I was pregnant when we moved to Truckee should have helped me make friends faster. After all, it's cool while you are pregnant. Strangers pay attention to you, open the door for you, love you for no reason. In addition to this royal treatment, you can eat anything you want because for the first time in your life, it is actually okay to be fat. In fact, if you are not fat, people worry about you. "Are you eating enough?" they ask if they haven't seen you with a Big Mac in your hand in the past five minutes.

"Here! Have another bowl of ice cream—you're eating for two!" they exclaim. It's bliss. But the catch is, the minute the baby is born, it's not cool to be fat anymore. And in my case, I had so much fun *getting* fat while I was pregnant that I was still fat for a good six months after the baby arrived.

One cannot underestimate how uncool carrying around an extra twenty postnatal pounds, largely in one's belly, can make a person feel. To illustrate: Once, I went out to dinner with Lance about a month after my son, Wilson, was born. I was still dressed in my maternity clothes because I could not get my right toe into anything I had worn before I got pregnant. I had at least bothered to put on makeup for the first time in two months, reasoning that if I made my face look nice, nobody would notice that from the neck down, I had the body of Santa Claus. Convinced by my own logic, I was genuinely shocked when a stranger walked up to me and said, "Congratulations! When are you due?" (For the record, this is the worst possible question you can ask a woman who is not pregnant.) I burst into tears, ran out of the restaurant, and left Lance to explain to the poor man that, in fact, I had already delivered our baby but had failed to deliver my fat.

The next time around, I was nobody's fool. I planned our second child so he would be born at the beginning of winter, in a ski town on top of a mountain. The timing and environment were such that I would have eight months to get my body into shape before I had to appear in a bathing suit. This strategy worked like a charm. After I gave birth to Oliver, I dressed in thick sweaters so people couldn't tell if I was fat or just bundled up for warmth. I wore more layers than a chocolate cake. I spent the entire winter sweating like a pig, but at least nobody asked me when I was due.

The bad thing about having a baby in Truckee was that my loneliness was exacerbated. Because we had only lived there a short time, I didn't have any friends at all in Truckee (except relatives, who don't count, because they have to hang out with you); therefore, nobody but my sister and her family and my mom came to see our new baby after he was born. As I was filling out Oliver's baby book when we returned home from the hospital, I burst into tears because there were at least twenty lines to list visitors on one of the pages. After I listed everyone in my extended family (individually so as to take up more space), I still had a half page left over. "Nobody has come to visit my baby!" I sniffed, swimming in the rush of hormones and fatigue that only newborns can inflict. I have the sneaking suspicion that my mother went door to door after that, looking for someone whom she could pay to come visit us and sign our glaringly empty baby book. Suspiciously, a neighbor I had met only once before stopped by to see Oliver a couple of days after my crying jag. She hadn't been in the door two seconds when she blurted out, "Do you have a baby book I can sign?" I glared at my mother and handed the book to the neighbor.

"Just turn to page twenty-three," my mom instructed, hovering over the woman while she scribbled her name. I sat sullenly on the sofa, like a teenager on a parentally organized, and very awkward, blind date.

Not much is more embarrassing than having your sixty-year-old mother go door to door, scrounging up friends for you. Because I didn't even trust my mom's taste in clothes and had returned almost every sweater she had ever bought me for Christmas, I didn't want her picking out an actual human being for me. In my experience, humans tend to be final sale only, and can't be returned.

No, I would have to pick out my own friends, and be choosy in the process, so I joined the Truckee

Family Connection, a group that organizes play dates for new mothers. I had resisted doing this because joining a mother's group to meet a buddy felt like joining a singles group to meet a guy. By virtue of the fact I was there at all, it would be obvious that I was lonely and desperate. But I was long past the point of being uncomfortable with the labels "lonely" and "desperate," so I decided to give it a try. It was interesting to learn (now that I was one) that grossly unpopular people don't aspire to be in the cool group. They aspire to be in *a* group—any group. I would be friends with all the other lonely, desperate people and be thankful for it.

I call to ask directions to the house of the woman who is hosting the play date. The woman's house is also on top of a mountain, albeit a different mountain than mine.

Already, we have something in common, I think. *I will make a friend!* I will find the other un-athletic people in Truckee who like to shop and have lunch instead of train for the self-imposed middle-aged Olympics. I pull all the way up her icy steep driveway, suddenly confident, and park by the front door. I go in. A group of women with babies on their laps are sitting around a kitchen table.

Children are running around everywhere, and it seems unbearably warm to me as I enter and put Oliver down on the floor in his car seat. I am sweating already but am too vain to take off my vest. If this get-together were in the city, I would be considered dressed down—dressed way down. I am wearing an outfit I might have thought was too casual to wear to Home Depot in the city, but in Truckee, I look like I am ready for a wedding. I am holding a fake designer handbag with logos all over it. I sense my mistake immediately. The other mothers have on no makeup, and of course, everyone is dressed in workout clothes.

"Hi. I'm Karly," a woman introduces herself as she walks up. She does not have one ounce, or even a half ounce, of fat on her body and is wearing her ski tights and a Lycra shirt. Her baby looks about two months old, and she is bouncing the baby on her hip. "I'm friends with your sister."

"I can't believe I actually know someone here," I squeal.

I have heard about Karly. She is a legend. She beat my brother-in-law in a 20k cross-country race last year, and he has not forgotten it. If my sister wants to make him mad, she just says, "I wonder if Karly wants to ski with us today," and he shuts up.

"So how are you liking Truckee?" she asks, eyeing my handbag.

"It's fake!" I want to scream. But they have all seen it. I have probably been branded as uppity, and it is too late to start over. In Truckee, the only acceptable name brands to flaunt are Patagonia and North Face, and I have disgraced myself by showing up like a poser with the unmistakably gaudy faux handbag of a French designer. To make matters worse, I am paying the price for owning something like this, and it is not even real. I am a double poser!

"Truckee is great," I lie. It's not a total lie. Parts of it are great. It's just that Truckee seems to amplify all my weaknesses and insecurities, and I hadn't planned for that. I hadn't even realized I was un-athletic and depended on my friends for happiness until I had left them all behind, after all.

Karly interrupts my reverie to tell me she is leaving to work out, and nobody else seems interested in talking to me; I have lost the desire to talk, anyway. It's too much work. The other mothers are all huddled around, gossiping about one of the new ski instructors in town. Apparently, she is having a raging affair with someone's husband. I am interested in this because though I can't ski well, I am a gold medalist in gossip.

Nobody is making room for me to join the talking circle, however, and I am self-conscious about hanging over the table like some sort of conversation voyeur. Oliver is asleep in his car seat, so I ask for the bathroom, where I spend ten minutes sitting on the counter. Finally, I hear Oliver crying and have to leave my hideout to help him.

I don't think anyone notices I have been gone, but I wonder if after I leave, I will be remembered as the sweaty chick with the over-the-top handbag who abandoned her son to hang out in the bathroom for half of the morning.

"Oliver feels a little warm," I say to no one, to the room. Children are running around, screaming and jumping on furniture, so nobody can hear me, anyway. "He might have a fever," I say louder, justifying my impending departure, which will go unnoticed.

As I leave the house, I see a long line of cars parked behind mine. Panic washes over me. Because I was early to the play date, I am trapped! I walk back into the house with heavy steps. I put Oliver's car seat back on the floor and sit down on the futon. Unless I ask every single person to move her car, I will be here for another hour, at least.

"Oliver is feeling better, so I came back," I explain to an unconcerned little girl whose nose is running with thick green mucus mixing with the chocolate around her mouth. I survey the crowd for someone, anyone, to talk to. The gossip circle is still deep in conversation at the kitchen table. On the outskirts is another fringe mother wondering whether to penetrate the inner sanctum. At first, I can see only her back. Like almost everyone else, she is wearing workout clothes. She is short and muscular, with long blonde hair. I consider approaching her. She turns around to face me.

As I recall the scene now, months later, it seems as if she turned to face me in slow motion. In my memory, I am like a bird flying outside my body, suspended over the play date. I watch myself from above, recoiling in horror, as I realize that the front of her hair is short. Very short. Hmm. Long hair in the back, plus short hair in the front equals—oh…my…God. She has a mullet. And not just any old mullet. She has the mother of all mullets: "Business in the front, party in the back." Hockey hair. A mullet so vintage that I haven't seen anything like it since White Snake played the Birmingham, Alabama, Civic Center in 1982.

"Don't be so shallow!" I tell myself. "Don't judge someone by their hairdo! What if someone is judging you because you are fifteen (okay, twenty) pounds overweight?"

I walk forward to say hello, trying to beat back a judgmental part of myself that I hate. She pivots to face me, looks at my fake bag, turns on her heel and walks off. When she is a safe distance from me she quickly pretends she is busy with her diaper bag.

Finally, people start to leave. The host of the play date extricates herself from the gossip circle and comes over to introduce herself to me. "I'm Joni," she says. "I'm so sorry we didn't get a chance to chat."

"Oh, me too." I smile. "I had a great time. Thank you so much for hosting us," I say, backing out of the door.

The other women brush past me without a word. Mullet knocks my pariah purse on the ground as she walks out, but doesn't apologize. Was it an accident? As we sat on opposite sides of the room pretending not to judge each other, she might have been wondering how anyone could think it was cool to wear that pretentious garb. Maybe for Mullet, my expensive purse was the deal breaker that told her our relationship could go no further.

I left the Truckee Family Connection without making any connections for my family. It turns out it is hard to make friends when you lock yourself in the bathroom and make superficial judgments about people you don't even know. But the upside is that I did learn a very valuable lesson: Never, ever, park at the front of someone's driveway during a party.

Gods and Whores

*T*ruckee is like an expensive call girl for tourists. It offers fun, but at a steep price. Reno, on the other hand, is a cheap whore. Houses that cost $1,000,000 in Truckee cost $300,000 in Reno. A box of cereal costs five dollars in Truckee, but you can score the same cereal for half the price in Reno. Whatever Truckee wants you to pay, Reno will give it to you for less, so whenever I feel a consumer itch, I head down to Reno to scratch it. About forty-five minutes away by car from the natural beauty of Truckee, Reno is so different from Truckee it may as well be on another planet. The Reno experience is one hundred percent man-made.

Crossing over the Nevada border from California, the landscape changes from scenic evergreen-covered foothills to a vast expanse of desert. Sandy hills pockmarked with dry, scrubby sagebrush stretch for miles. As you descend to the flat valley floor, billboards advertising free steak dinners and the "loosest slots" at casinos appear on the horizon, along with signs imploring you to "EXIT NOW!" for complimentary gas and truck-stop jackpots. About ten minutes before you enter the Reno city limits, Boomtown, a fake old west town built in the 1980s, appears like a Disneyland–style mirage to thirsty gamblers on the side of the highway. Its flashing lights and pastel Wild West facade lure those so eager to try their luck that they pull over, too impatient to drive the few miles to the larger casinos in town.

If you do make it into town, you'll see look-alike apartment complexes perched on the bald hillsides, and cheap motel rooms flanking the highway, their doors guarding dirty secrets like endless rows of soldiers at attention. Mini storage lots and piles of scrap metal stand next to dumps filled with old tires. Behind the highway's concrete sound barrier, the roofs of trailers housing illegal immigrants, card dealers, and broke retirees peep at the white stretch limos whizzing by. Reno isn't hiding anything; Her seedy underbelly lies faceup for all to see.

The Reno Chamber of Commerce calls Reno "the biggest little city in America," but locals know it by a more appropriate slogan: "Poor Man's Vegas." Like the musicians and strippers who perform inside them, the casinos are worn out and past their prime. Ever wonder where Engelbert Humperdinck or Menudo went? Chances are, they are on tour in Reno. It's where bands from the '70s and '80s come to die. Even the Peppermill, commonly known as the nicest casino in town, is twenty years overdue for a remodel. Its faded gold railings and dim blue lights depress rather than titillate. But tourists crowd in nonetheless, looking for a little excitement. Throngs of salesmen at conventions kill time by watching sagging women take off their clothes. They don't seem to mind that upon closer look, it's all a little low-rent. The lap dances cost $100 less than in Vegas, so it doesn't matter if the strippers are uglier, as long as the lights are low.

 I can't judge these guys for paying for pleasure, because I treat Reno like a cheap stripper, myself. I come in, throw money at her, take what I need, and leave. I'm not much of a gambler, so the casinos aren't typically my destination. No, I have an addiction of a different sort, which Reno is only too happy to enable. My vice isn't strippers; it's strip malls. And Reno supplies them plentifully. The thing about Reno is, she makes everything so easy. If you want to get drunk, you can find a bar on any highway exit. If you want to gamble or pay for sex, you can do that at almost any highway exit, too.

Reno isn't proud like Truckee. She doesn't have to mark up her offerings and sell them at quaint, scenic boutiques and tourist traps. No, Reno is all about volume and availability.

I find this liberating, and it's why I like strip malls. I don't want an overzealous saleswoman breathing down my neck, asking if she can help me pick out my toothpaste. I want to be anonymous. I want to go in a store, fill my basket to the rim in record time, pay, and leave. The only contact I need with other people is the brief impact of skin on skin as I hand the cashier my credit card. I'm not saying this to be rude—it's just that interrupting me while I am shopping is like talking to someone while they are praying. Shopping is a spiritual pursuit for me, and I want to commune directly with my god.

Now, I'm as monotheistic as any good Christian, Jew, or Muslim. In the religion of strip-mall shopping, there is only one god. The source of the most complete consumer fulfillment, the Alpha and the Omega of bargain purchases, is Target. And Reno is not home to just any Target; she is home to the Greatland Target, a store so massive that it takes up three whole addresses at the Pioneer Way Shopping Center. As I exit off South Virginia Street into the Target parking lot, I hear angels sing. Butterflies flutter to and fro in my stomach, alerting me to the assured consumer satisfaction that lies ahead. What myriad impulse purchases will I make today? What beautiful but useless designer desk toys and DVDs will find their way to my shopping cart?

But before I can worship I need a miracle: I must find a place to park. And the parking lot is vast—a veritable desert to be crossed. I am arriving at midday, and the shady spots under the thirsty, drooping trees are already taken. I park at the end of the lot and begin my trek, a journey that is not for the spiritually weak. The parking lot is a frying pan, the hot desert sun beating down on the cars and customers with relentless fury. Sweat rolls off my skin like water, and I become as lightheaded as a Native American in a sweat hut. Nature is purifying me for my own spirit quest in the cool, numbered aisles of the Great One.

As I grab a cart and breeze through the automatic doors, euphoria washes over me. I feel at peace and alive. The shoppers here are my sisters and brothers, fellow pilgrims on a quest for consumer enlightenment. So what if I am the only person I can see who doesn't have a bold, obvious, and sort of scary tattoo? I belong here. I break right and work through the store counterclockwise, my usual rotation. I begin to pray.

Designer Post-it notes with matching pencil holder—*sold!* Ten rolls of gift wrap with coordinating ribbons—*sold!* Smoothie maker—*cool!* Spongebob sippy cups, Spongebob underwear, Spongebob sponges—*The kids will love these!* A year's worth of Swiffer products—*I'll finally get the house clean. Sold!* I am buying so much stuff, I'll need some plastic tubs to get organized—ten giant Rubbermaid boxes—*sold!*

And then, panic. My cart is overflowing, and I haven't even made it to the pharmacy section. I need diapers, shampoo, lotion, Band-Aids, and toothbrushes in every color of the rainbow.

Mystics have revealed that when one is in the midst of a spiritual revelation, one becomes unaware of the passage of time. Such is my experience in Target. I look at my watch and am surprised to find that I have been here two hours already. I must tear myself away. I need to get home in time for dinner, and I have two more stops to make. So many strip malls, so little time!

I grab a super-sized Coke on my way out the door. I will need some energy for the next two stores. Although shopping at several strip malls in one day is exhilarating, it's also really tiring—sort of similar to having sex three times in a row.

My next stop is an organic market. When you hear "organic," you think of hippies, nature lovers, and vegetarians, right? Not in Reno! The staff of the Wild Oats market in Reno appears to be comprised entirely of former hookers and pole dancers. On today's trip, as I stand in the checkout line, I have to be reminded by the cashier to scan my credit card because I am so busy gaping at the woman bagging my groceries. She is of average height and appears to be about seventy-five years old. I can't be sure if that is her actual age because it appears that hard living combined with the dry desert and hot sun has added years to this woman's skin. What's funny is, she is also staring at me. I look down at my shirt and realize that the Carl's Jr. burger I dropped on myself at lunch has made a big ketchup stain near my breast. I reach to cover it with my hand, and realize I am shaking like a drug addict, because the super-sized soda I drank at Target has hit me like a pound of meth. God knows what she thinks of me. I am wearing a scrunchy in my hair today (circa 1988), and I didn't bother putting on makeup. But she isn't the only one thinking catty thoughts. Evidently, nobody has informed her she stopped looking good in a mini skirt about thirty years ago. Her legs are rail thin, and the skin hangs on them like an anorexic elephant's. She is beyond tan, the color of sierra mud. A denim skirt with a frayed hem hangs about six inches above her knees, and dirty tennis shoes hide her cracked feet. Her hair is the yellow white color of a lifetime peroxide habit and has the rough texture of an old horse's tail. I can tell that her eyes used to be beautiful, but now they are a washed-out hazel color and appear to be lined by a thick, black Sharpie marker. She smiles at me.

"Paper or plastic, darling?" she barks in a husky voice through nicotine-yellowed teeth.

"Paper," I respond.

I can imagine her saying, "Blow job or sex, honey?" and wonder if that ever slips out her mouth by accident as she piles carton after carton of eggs and milk into grocery bags.

After my third stop, I am starting to crash from my high, so I rush out of town and across the state line like a bootlegger with illegal contraband. I peek in my backseat at the pile of bags from Target and automatically feel a sense of shame about my binge, as well as (oddly enough) the beginning of a longing for another chain-store run. I didn't even have time to go to the mall, after all! I vow to hold my urge at bay for at least a week; I need time to recover physically from my excursion.

The cheapest trip I can make to Reno is a trip to the airport, where, again, retired strippers and hookers stream into the workforce. Every time I am at the airport, I see several of them working the newsstands or the airport casino's cash desk or sweeping up paper towels in the ladies' room. You can tell they are former ladies of the night because they still dress as if they are headed to their old jobs: stiletto heels, tight pants, and tank tops showing sagging cleavage and withered flesh. Once a night owl, always a night owl, I suppose, because it's usually when I am stuck waiting for someone at the airport late at night when I see these women the most.

On the inside, the Reno airport looks like any other airport in America, except for the jingling bells and flashing lights on the slot machines. You didn't think Reno would miss a chance to take your money, did you? Bored or weary travelers looking to kill time are the target audience at the Reno airport, and in that respect it's a little less depressing than some of the lifers you see playing slots at a casino. At least when you are gaming in the airport, your neighbor at the slot machine next to you hasn't got silver fingers from pumping quarters into the machine for ten hours straight. At least you don't have to worry whether the old lady beside you has just blown her Social Security check and is living out of her car.

When Reno whores come up to Truckee, they are easy to pick out. They are the only women not dressed in hiking boots and fleece jackets. And they are even easier to spot when they show up at the neighborhood pool, as was the case in Truckee recently. The Truckee Police Department is not often tasked with solving major crimes. Read the crime report in the local paper any week, and you'll find several incidences of public drunkenness, bears breaking into garbage cans, and, if it is a really interesting week, a TV stolen from someone's vacation house, so when the body of a dead woman stuffed in a large duffel bag ended up in the parking lot of a resort's swimming pool parking lot, the whole town was set on its ear. Two golfers found the duffel bag near their car as they came in from playing eighteen holes one day. One of them unzipped the bag, assuming someone had accidentally left luggage on the way out of town. Imagine the poor man's shock at finding a face inside—a dead hooker's face, to be precise—along with the rest of her very dead body.

The neighborhood went into a frenzy. Choppers buzzed overhead, and policemen set up a road block, questioning everyone who came into and out of the neighborhood. Beyond being concerned for their immediate safety, homeowners secretly worried if the arrival of this unfortunate piece of baggage would adversely affect their property values. It was safe to assume that a suitcase-wielding ax murderer would not do a whole lot for asking prices in the area.

Police as well as local residents were relieved to hear, upon receipt of the autopsy report, that the woman (later identified as a drug user and prostitute by some of her homeless friends in Reno) had likely died of a heart attack rather than foul play. However, stuffing someone who died of natural causes in a duffel bag and dumping them in a parking lot, as it turns out, is a crime in and of itself. Police suspected that someone had hired the woman and she had died of heart failure while performing her duties. The john had then panicked, realizing that if he called the police, his dirty secret would be out. To this day, the mystery remains unsolved, but I think about it every time I pull into the parking lot of the pool to take a swim. I am careful not to leave my giant beach bag lying around, as I wouldn't want to frighten anyone unnecessarily.

In many ways, I am no different from the john. For one thing, it seems that we frequent the same swimming pool. Beyond that, we both like to pick up things in Reno and bring them back to Truckee in bags. Granted, I am only bringing back groceries and whatever Target has on sale, but the john and I both understand that Reno is Truckee's great enabler: Whatever our addictions, she'll supply us, no questions asked.

Are We Having Fun Yet?

When I am sitting in my pajamas, having breakfast, skiing seems like a good idea. After all, it's a winter wonderland outside. A storm blew through last night and dumped six inches of fresh snow, covering everything in a pristine, sparkling white blanket. The sky is a startling cloudless turquoise. Looking out the kitchen window, I squint. The glare temporarily blinds me. Though I glance outside for only a moment, I see spots before my eyes. I have to put on sunglasses to eat my Cheerios.

Lance saunters into the kitchen, smiling. "It's a bluebird," he beams. ("Bluebird" is skier-speak for a perfect blue sky the morning after a storm.)

"Hurry up and have your breakfast so we can get out there," I urge.

No sooner have I uttered the words than I am amazed they actually came out of my mouth. I am beginning to realize I may be suffering from a horribly serious medical condition. I not only suffer from it but am also the person who has discovered it. (A dubious distinction that many hypochondriacs may claim.) Its symptoms appear like this: Each time I go out to ski, I have forgotten that I actually hate to ski. What's more, the suggestion to go skiing is frequently my idea. My self-diagnosis? Ski amnesia, or skinesia (a word I have made up but am hoping will catch on). This syndrome must be contagious, and I am quite sure I have infected poor Lance. You see, each time he agrees to ski with me, he has forgotten that I always whine and complain until I convince him to abandon the slopes. Maybe ten percent of the time, the ski gods are with me and I feel competent and able to stick with it for almost an hour, but ninety percent of the time, I want to feign an injury so I can go back to the lodge and have hot chocolate.

Today I feel a slight sense of dread before I even don my Lycra tights and boots. This is not a good sign. Sports psychologists might call this negative anticipation. I am anticipating a negative performance and thus am likely to perform negatively. We are going cross-country skiing, a task that looks easy but is actually not. One would think that because the cross-country skier is gliding across a flat surface rather than skiing down a steep slope, not much skill would be involved.

"That looks easy!" Lance proclaimed before signing up for lessons a couple of years ago. "If I can walk, I should be able to cross-country ski."

Although skiing seems as easy as walking to him, it is definitely not the case for me. It's a little embarrassing, actually. Lance is from Mississippi—not exactly a Nordic environment. The biggest hill in Mississippi is about nine feet above sea level, and Lance didn't see snow until he went to college in the Northeast. In fact, the first time he ever went downhill skiing, he was twenty years old. He broke his leg in his first five minutes on skis, when some unforgiving bindings refused to release and he fell so hard, he heard his fibula and tibia snap in half. You'd think this would have discouraged him, but instead, when we started dating, he was raring to try it again. Ten years after his painful winter break, he was off and gliding as if he'd been skiing all his life. Though I had been skiing fifteen years longer than he had, within two weeks, he was a better skier than I was. I should have been happy for him, right? After all, my true love had stared down his demons and conquered his fears. I definitely should have been happy for him. But I wasn't. I was annoyed. How could he be better than I was so soon? I hadn't even had time to gloat! It really wasn't fair. I only had one week to act superior and charitable before he was skiing in front of me, playing coach and giving me pointers.

I think Lance and I have a good marriage because the only time I really hate him is when we are skiing. On the cross-country trails, he usually cruises ahead and then skis back to catch up with me. He does this for the entire run, managing to keep his heart rate up though I am making progress at a turtle's speed. I am not sure if it is to motivate me or chastise me, but along the way, he frequently makes underhanded comments like "You look like you are afraid of falling today," or "Is there something wrong with your equipment?"

Today, the trail has not been groomed yet, so the snow is fluffy and powdery and my skis sink in it. Each time I try to get traction to glide, one ski sticks and my body lurches forward over my legs. I struggle not to fall, but I can't help it. We've been out less than fifteen minutes, and I have lost my balance and tumbled backward twice. Each time I fall, I have to wiggle my skis out from under the deep snow while somehow managing to keep my own leg bones from snapping. There is a reason God did not make our feet six feet long. If you have ever had skis stuck in deep snow, you know it is similar to being tied to giant two-by-fours and buried in cold peanut butter. Pulling your legs and skis out and getting them parallel so you can stand up is an athletic feat.

Not ten minutes into our outing today, I've fallen again, and, growing increasingly irrational, I pray for a rescue party. I turn around to see if anyone is coming. In the distance, I spot someone skiing in my direction. Perhaps I am hallucinating, like a thirsty wanderer in the desert who thinks she sees water. Maybe it is a hot guy in a ski-patrol outfit heading my way. I wait expectantly, ready to burst into tears and throw myself in the helpful stranger's arms. As the figure edges closer, my hot guy turns into a fifty-year-old woman who gives me a look of pity and cruises up the hill behind me. I am left alone with my reality. I have a large blob of snow down my pants, my rear end is wet and frozen, and I want to go home.

Soon Lance is back on on one of his boomerang trajectories. "It's awesome out here," he yells to me, and moves ahead with the force of a snowplow barreling down the trail.

"Are you f**king kidding me?" I yell back. Either he does not hear me or he has chosen to ignore me. If he has chosen to ignore me, I don't blame him. I want to ignore me, too. I can't be driving him any more crazy than I am driving myself. For every complaint I utter out loud, I utter ten more silently in my head. "I am so cold my fingertips are numb," I do not say. "My ski boots are too small, and my toes are so squished together, my toenails are cutting my toes," I do not say. Lance has disappeared from the horizon. I am jealous. I want to leave me, too. I visualize skiing down the trail, past Lance, into the valley, and back up the hill. I want to know what it is like to be good at this, to ski so well and so beautifully that I actually enjoy it. I am tired of trying all the time. I want it to be effortless. I want to feel like a champion; I want to ski like Picabo Street. But more than anything at all, I want to get the snow out of my underwear.

 Lance is skiing toward me now, a silver-jacketed blur in the distance bulleting ahead with the grace of a racehorse. He is working hard, his breath steaming as his legs rock back and forth, skating over the snow. I can see his red face clearly now, grinning and dripping with sweat.

 "Are you getting your heart rate up?" he asks with fake concern. He has already turned around and is headed away from me again.

 I may not be getting my heart rate up, but I feel my blood pressure rise. I secretly will him to face-plant. I don't wish him severe bodily injury, just severe humiliation. I would like to order up one ABC Wide World of Sports "agony of defeat" moment. He has experienced the "thrill of victory" enough already. I want him to tumble end over end until the tops of his skis are buried in snow and he is stuck in a facedown snow angel. Then I will go and pick him up, help him dust the snow from his face, and ask, "Is there something wrong with your equipment?"

Skiing is like gossiping or drinking too much: It brings out the worst in me, but I do it anyway. I know I shouldn't, but I just can't help it. I forget how bad it makes me feel, so I continue repeating the corrosive behavior. Lance must really love me, because he sees this ugly cycle repeat itself every winter and still, he does not file for divorce. He does not even bring up my bad behavior to make me feel guilty. This is yet another way he and I are different.

"You always ski off and leave me!" I shout to him. He is a dot on the horizon in front of me. While he waits for me, he kills time by knocking snow off of tree branches with his ski poles. I wonder if he is so mad at me that he has to take it out on the tree limbs, pretending each one is my leg or my arm or my snarling, pissed-off face. I wonder if he feels better when he whacks each branch and feels the snow explode and rain down like flakey white fireworks.

As I approach Lance, I ski harder and faster. I am so angry from these thoughts that my fury propels me forward. The faster I reach him, the faster we can get in a fight. I am ready to win this one! I am ready to end this failed outing with some fireworks of my own. On the trail about twenty yards from Lance, I make out a shape. I am guessing he has written a rude remark about me in the snow. When I ski up to it, I see a big heart traced lovingly with the end of his ski pole. Inside is written L + E = love. Though my rear end is still frozen, I suddenly feel warm inside. My heart thaws along with my anger. Instantly, I love him again. There can't be another man on the planet who could love this ski bitch.

I ski over to him and give him a big hug. At the end of the trail, the plow has left a high mound of snow over the curb where our car is parked. I will have to jump down it in my skis to get home. I am so traumatized, I am now scared even of this.

"I can't do it," I whisper to Lance.

"Yes, you can!" he says. "Don't think about it. Just go."

He holds my hand as I bend my knees and jump down over the curb to our car. I do not fall! *Victory!* In my inner Olympics, I give myself a gold medal in the Curb-Jumping event. As we drive home, I actually find myself looking forward to our next ski outing, a sure sign my skinesia remains incurable.

Truckee Time

*P*eople in Truckee don't worry too much about time because there is always plenty of it. As East Coasters moving to this sleepy town, Lance and I soon learned we were type-A aliens from another planet, invading the land of the perpetually calm and relaxed. For us, time was precious. It was not to be wasted. After all, in our experience, time was money. For Truckeeites, time only matters when it concerns what *time* the chairlifts are opening or what *time* everyone is meeting at the Bar of America for a round of beer.

You might think construction contractors in big cities are notorious for ignoring time and running late with their building projects, but they seem like Swiss watches compared to their small-town Truckee counterparts. Nothing could frustrate a couple of time-conscious East Coast transplants more than a builder in Truckee. Here, contractors don't need to worry about time, because as our sleepy little railroad town transforms into a resort mecca, the builders are getting rich. They can spend $500,000 building a house and sell it for $2,000,000. Not bad earnings, by anyone's standards. So trying to get a contractor to do small jobs for small fees at your house is like trying to hire U2 to play at your prom. This means the people left to perform the odd jobs are the home-improvement equivalent of professional wedding singers. They aren't good enough to make it onto the big jobs, but they'll show up at your house and charge you rock-star rates to do mediocre jobs. This is how we ended up with Chad, the man-boy landscaper who became the bane of our existence. Chad taught us what "Truckee time" really is.

When we moved into our brand-new house, our front yard was nothing more than a large heap of dirt. We needed excavation work, and lots of it. We would need to have dirt moved by the types of heavy machinery that only my two-year-old son could name.

"Excavators and earthmovers and backhoes!" Wilson squealed as Lance and I pondered how to get the giant mountain of mud out of our front yard. I placed six calls to landscapers whose numbers I found in the yellow pages, and only one returned our call (two weeks later). I was so thrilled that someone finally responded to our desperate plea, I was willing to hire him before I even met him. That was how Chad got the job.

We were supposed to meet at ten a.m., so when Chad rolled into the driveway at noon that day, I already hated him. But I needed him, so I couldn't fire him. This is how our entirely dysfunctional relationship began.

"Hey, what's up?" a tall blonde guy around twenty-five years old said as I opened the door. He looked and sounded like a surfer who had gotten lost on the way to the beach and ended up in the mountains. He smiled broadly and did not apologize for being late. I decided to point out his error in a passive-aggressive way. I didn't want to be directly rude, because if he ran for the hills, I would really be stuck in the mud.

"Oh, I thought you were showing up at ten?" I asked in a sweet voice.

"Oh, dude, it's already twelve?" he marveled, genuinely amazed, looking at his watch. (I was surprised he even owned a watch. Most people around here don't, and if they do, it is only so they can monitor their pulses while they are running up the side of a cliff.) "I was out skiing the corn at Squaw this morning," he explained, as if this provided him amnesty for whatever wrong he may have committed. (The icy spring snowpack called corn among the locals is best skied in the morning and, as such, tends to delay all actual work until later in the day, when the corn gets slushy.) "It was awesome at first, but then it was like, mash potatoes all of a sudden, so I decided to come up here."

"That was really generous of you," I said sarcastically. This was not a charity job, after all. I was sure I would soon be forking over an outrageous sum of money.

"Oh, yeah, no problem," he said, completely oblivious to my sarcasm.

After Chad assured me he could make my hill of dirt look like a front yard "in two weeks, max," I grudgingly gave him the job. Sure enough, heavy equipment lumbered up the hill in front of our house the very next morning, and the people driving them worked hard, for at least two hours. Then they took a four-hour lunch break. And then it was time to go home. The work "day" went on like this for a week, and then, at the beginning of the second week, nobody showed up at all.

"Chad? Are you there?" I seethed as I left him my third voice mail of the day. "Nobody showed up today, and I just wanted to let you know that." I had met some of the guys with the long lunch breaks the week before and had learned that Chad had created an instant workforce by hiring his friends. They, like him, thought nothing of abandoning a day of work to eke out some of the last skiing of the season.

The next day, and for the rest of the week, nobody showed up and nobody returned my calls. I had given Chad a fifty percent down payment for the work, but I hadn't expected him to complete fifty percent of the job. Faced with a now level field of mud and a multitude of unreturned calls to Chad, as well as to all of the people I had called to finish the job so I could fire Chad, I sat stewing in my resentment.

"This would never happen on the East Coast!" I ranted to Lance. "People *want* to work there! They actually show up for their jobs and earn their paychecks!" Suddenly, I had forgotten everything bad about the East Coast: the rudeness, the dirty air, the cramped housing, the endless traffic jams. These were all the things that we had wanted to escape, that had compelled us to move in the first place. We just hadn't known that the opposite of all these things would be so unbelievably annoying: the perpetual laid-back attitude, the aggressive friendliness, the need to ski more than work, the complete lack of urgency about anything at all.

I checked my answering machine every five minutes for the next two weeks, praying that someone, anyone, had called me back so I could fire Chad, but my hoped-for replacements must also have been out skiing corn, because my little red light only beeped with calls from my sister and my mother, who were calling for a daily update on the disappearing-Chad saga.

And then, about three weeks after I had abandoned all hope of ever staring out at anything but a mud pit, I heard a rumbling sound coming up the street. It was late, around eleven p.m., on Friday night. I looked outside, and the eerie lights of an eighteen-wheeler shone onto our driveway. A small furtive man with the look of a gopher opened the back doors of the trailer and began to unload plants: aspens and arctic willows and lavender, followed by daisies and black-eyed susans and Russian sage, silver leaves shining in the moonlight. I ran out in my slippers to ask the covert plant deliveryman who he was. Was he an angel sent from nursery heaven to rescue me from my horticultural nightmare? Did he have any connection to Chad whatsoever? Was he here to answer a desperate homeowner's prayer?

"Is Chad ever coming back?" I whispered to the ghostly apparition in our driveway.

The mysterious man just shrugged, climbed back into the eighteen-wheeler, and headed back down the mountain.

I had high hopes that Chad would appear the next morning as mysteriously and benevolently as the plants had the night before, but alas, it was not to be. The plants sat in my yard, in their plastic buckets, for at least two weeks. Every morning, I ran around watering them, hoping they would survive.

I resigned myself to the fact that someday, Chad would show up as mysteriously as the plant delivery angel and that I was completely at his mercy. I had long since stopped leaving him messages; his answering machine sneered *"This mailbox is full!"* at me every time I tried.

Six weeks after the plants arrived, he finally showed up, making no mention of the month-long lapse or the unreturned calls.

"Umm, Chad," I said calmly, having spent all my anger in imagined conversations with him in the bathroom mirror, "I thought this job was going to be finished four weeks ago."

"Oh yeah," he said. "I got really busy on another job, and your place is just so far from my house. Sometimes it's hard to motivate to come up here."

This behavior would have been unacceptable anywhere but in Truckee. Here, it was common, even expected. "Hard to motivate" and "skiing corn" were probably excused absences in the local school. "So why didn't you return any of my calls?" I asked.

"Hey, don't you know guys don't like talking on the phone?" He smiled, trying to charm his way out of the situation.

"I'm not trying to date you, Chad," I hissed. "I'm trying to employ you. And that means when I leave you a message, you need to call me back."

He took a step away from me. "Well, I hired some of my bros to come up here and finish this up, but I just got a postcard from them. Seems they decided to head down to Chile to do some carving in the pow pow down there. There's no froshie here anymore, and a dude starts to feel like he's starving for it after a month or so. We've only got Sierra cement now," he sighed mournfully as he cast a longing glance at the last remnants of the spring snowpack on a neighboring peak.

I was a novice at translating ski lingo, but I gathered this to mean that his crew had abandoned my project to ski powder in Chile because the snow here had melted. I took this as more evidence that I had overpaid Chad, if his staff could afford to take vacations that I could only dream of.

Anger bubbled inside me like a Chilean volcano. I could be passive- aggressive no more. I would have to tell Chad how angry I was and tell him now. The risk that he would not show up for the job if I shared my true feelings was gone.

"Chad, here's how it is going to be," I said. "If you have any hope of getting paid for these plants that are out here dying of thirst in the hot sun, you are going to show up every day for the next two weeks and finish this job like you said you would over a month ago. Otherwise, I am not going to pay you a red cent. Do you understand?"

"Chill," he said, amazed that I was upset. "It's under control. I'll get it done."

"Don't tell me to chill!" I shrilled. "I have had it with your lax attitude and your disappearing ski-bum friends!"

"Relax," he said. "We're all on Truckee time here, didn't you know that? That's why they call it Flake Tahoe!" he laughed as I turned my back and went inside.

In the end, my two-week project took months to complete. We paid Chad only half of what we owed him, because of the emotional stress we incurred from wondering whether anyone was showing up day after day, and wondering whether snow would fall before the garden was finally planted. My experience with Chad left me feeling like I was slowly being driven crazy by a culture that was so relaxed. Like a clock sounding its alarm, the truth began to ring in my ears. Maybe Truckee was not the place for me. I could add "too impatient to live here" to my list of "too un-athletic to live here" and "too annoyed by deep snow to live here." It was time to think about moving on.

Moving On

*S*arah was experiencing a depression. To be specific, it was a tropical depression. Unseasonably warm weather had ridden in on the warm jet stream from the Pacific. The last month of the ski season was turning into a complete washout. Heavy rain saturated our previously pristine snowpack. With each passing day, more large clumps of grass peaked through the ski trails at the cross-country center. Weeks earlier, imperceptible to the skiers above, melting snow had begun to trickle into frozen creek beds, slowly awakening the sleeping streams beneath. Soon, cracks had formed on top of the snow, the water escaping and rushing freely for the first time in months. If you stood still and listened, you could hear the season changing. Chunks of ice and snow slipped off trees and thudded to the ground below. The constant dripping of water signaled the unmistakable sound of the thaw.

"You can't even get up Little Dipper now," Sarah stopped by to announce, as if I needed up-to-the-minute information on the demise of her favorite ski trail.

Standing in my kitchen, she was crestfallen. The melt was a month earlier than usual. It was only the beginning of April, and Sarah's plans to ski for at least another three weeks were dashed. Locals refer to this period of mud and un-skiable, un-bikeable terrain as the shoulder season. It signifies a slushy mess to be tolerated until warm summer weather arrives at the end of June and backcountry hiking and biking can fill the days until the first flakes fall again.

"The good news is, there is a twenty percent chance the precipitation today will freeze, because a small arctic blast is competing with the Pineapple Express flow from Hawaii," she said, sounding hopeful. "In fact, I think I hear something. Do you hear that pinging sound? Is that snow hitting the window?"

"I think that's the coffee percolating," I said. "Sorry to rain on your parade."

In Truckee, the only thing worse than no snow is rain. It makes whatever snow you have completely worthless and leaves the workout junkies with no way to exercise their itching muscles but the treadmill.

I reached out to touch her arm. "Sarah, I think it might be time to move on," I said gently. "Seasons change. We need to accept it."

The concept of moving on was on my mind a lot these days. Some months earlier, the thaw had begun in our own lives, also imperceptible at first. A weekend trip to San Francisco had left us missing city life. A job lead for Lance had turned into one interview and then another. A couple of months later, the interviews developed into a job offer in Seattle. By shoulder season, our resistance to the urban jungle we had been desperate to escape two years earlier had melted. We decided to go. After almost two years living at 7,000 feet, we were headed back to sea level and a big city.

When I told my sister that we were moving, she was confused. "Truckee is paradise," she said. "Why would anyone ever leave?"

But what was paradise for her, it turns out, was not paradise for me. I had moved to Truckee with the half-formed thinking of a little sister who thought she would like the same things as the older sister she idolized. In overvaluing how great it would be to live where Sarah lived and where we vacationed, I had undervalued my urban streak and the city things I actually like to do. I mean, sure, I like to hike. For a couple of hours. And on occasion, I like to ski, but only downhill on groomed intermediate slopes, and only on sunny to partly cloudy days with no wind. (I have worked out the exact conditions I need to ski in so that I do not morph into the Ski Bitch.)

It was easy for me to ignore parts of myself until I moved away from my friends and from city life and was made to confront those parts. Now I had to admit to my sister and to myself that I belonged where the trees grow right next to cement. I had discovered that the boots I like to wear aren't made for snow but have heels and look really good with short skirts.

Considering you can see grass for only four months a year in Truckee, I was focused on how the grass would be greener (year-round) in Seattle. I would no longer have to air my urban side in Reno, wallowing in Target like a pig in slop. In Seattle, I could actually live in a neighborhood where my neighbors resided in their houses year-round. Fewer than half of the houses in our neighborhood in Truckee were owned by full-time residents. Most are second homes occupied on select weekends or holidays. It was always lonely to look out of the window at night and realize that ours was the only house with the porch light on.

I was also looking forward to restaurants, shopping, and theater—all of the cultural attractions normally associated with life in the big city. Most of all, I was excited about making friends. I had forgotten what it was like to socialize with people who weren't former Olympians and who had hobbies besides working out. I was sure with a bigger selection of people to choose from, I would be able to find a few friends.

The funny thing was, after we had lived in Seattle for about six months, we often escaped the rainy weekends by going shopping at REI. We were looking for an outdoor fix, but it was too wet to enjoy the great outdoors. Ironically, it wasn't until months after I had been safely installed in my urban nest, children in preschool and boxes unpacked, that I could appreciate, and consequently miss, the part of Truckee that I loved—the part that had nothing to do with civilization. I woke up one rainy day in Seattle, craving the dry heat of the sierra. I missed the summer smell of dirt and evergreens and the rustling sound of dying wildflowers blowing under an August sun. I closed my eyes and remembered the blinding light of a crystal-blue day reflected on the snow. I heard the streams. I saw the view of Mt. Rose from our back deck. I wanted to walk out my front door, hike up to my favorite alpine lake, and breathe in the pure mountain air. I missed all of it: the peaks, the valleys, and, most of all, Sarah.

    Maybe it was time for a vacation.

CPSIA information can be obtained at www.ICGtesting.com
Printed in the USA
LVOW05s1948210714

395346LV00001B/2/P